BETH BLECHERMAN

MY PARENT

PLAN

HOW TO CREATE
A FAMILY PROJECT PLAN
TO ORGANIZE YOUR LIFE
AND YOUR KIDS

MY PARENT PLAN

How to Create a Family Project Plan to Organize Your Life and Your Kids

Beth Blecherman

Copyright © 2012 Beth Blecherman

ISBN-13: 978-1492147091
ISBN-10: 1492147095

All rights reserved. No part of this book may be reproduced or transmitted in any form by any means, electronic, mechanical, photocopying, recording, or otherwise, without the prior written permission of the publisher.

The information in this book is provided for informational purposes. Neither the publisher nor the author shall be liable for any physical, psychological, emotional, financial, or commercial damages, including but not limited to special, incidental, consequential or other damages caused or allegedly caused, directly or indirectly, by the use of the information in this book. The author and publisher specifically disclaim any liability incurred from the use or application of the contents of this book. Examples in this book are not all-inclusive and may not apply in every case; readers should seek professional advice for emergency preparedness, finances, and all other issues. Websites are subject to change.

Printed in the United States of America

DEDICATION

This book is dedicated to ever parent who has ever asked, "How can I prepare and manage my family schedule?" The information in this book will help you answer that question and plan for it. There are always surprises and challenges in raising children, but, with a parent plan, you'll be able to create the path to find solutions.

This book is also dedicated to my wonderful husband, three boys, parents and in-laws, and extended family and friends who not only supported me through my own parenting journey, but who are also the best village I could ask for. Special thanks to my husband for his invaluable support and feedback.

To BlogHer, Guy Kawasaki, and many other social media communities (listed in the resource section), for being the catalysts to connect me with the amazing "village" of social media entrepreneurs. Special thanks go to Kimberley Clayton Blaine, an early pioneer in creating a business in digital programming and social media, and other parent entrepreneurs for sharing ideas and inspiration.

To Alicia Dunams (http://www.aliciadunams.com) and her Bestseller in a Weekend team for not only helping me convert my ideas into a book plan, but also giving me the help I needed to move things forward while I kept my Techmamas.com business and three kids going strong. I am thankful she and her team were available and always had solutions for my questions when I felt like the obstacles of writing a book were too great to overcome.

To my production team: XFactorDesigns.com for my website/graphics, Siobhan Gallagher for editing and Babyjidesign.com for my headshot.

Last, this book is dedicated to every parent's journey into creating a parenting plan. This book won't tell you what your specific parenting plan should be, but it will help you travel through the process of developing your own.

TABLE OF CONTENTS

INTRODUCTION

I didn't have a plan when I had my first child, which some might find surprising, considering the fact that I was a project manager at the time. When I became a parent, I forgot everything I knew about planning. Overwhelmed, I listened to many different people tell me what to do as a parent. I bought tons of stimulating toys—admittedly, I was a toy and parenting information hoarder—and I lost touch with my child, myself, and my own understanding of what I needed. As a result, I made mistakes. However, I noticed that every time I returned to planning, I became more successful at parenting. Thus, the idea of project planning in parenting was born.

Through my experiences, I hope to help parents and families get the information they need to understand the process of creating a parent plan based on their individual family's needs and personalities. Different families have unique needs, so it's impossible to rely entirely on the advice and guidance of others. One parenting style does not fit all. Each person must understand and define their own needs, as well as the needs of their family, so they can transfer those needs into a process and plan customized for them. Once the process is in place, it will help families get through the inevitable struggles and challenges as they go through different stages in their lives. With each phase, they'll learn and grow and be able to update their plan so that when surprises occur—and they will—they'll be able to handle them without asking, "Oh, my, what am I going to do now?"

With a parent plan, you'll never have to step back and say, "If I had just planned for that, I could have done it." You'll have the assurance that, regardless of what happens, you can be ready to respond in a way that's best for you and your family. That makes for a happy parent and happy children—it also helps you understand your family's dynamic better and integrate it into your plan. Once you create your plan, you can step away and engage with your family, comfortable in knowing your next steps. Or, when obstacles, life changes, or surprises come your way, as they do with every parent, you can step back and create a new plan.

In my past role as a consulting manager, I created project plans to manage technology implementations. In my role as a technologist on my site TechMamas.com, I help parents integrate technology into parenting. Technology can make parenting much easier, but only if you know your family's needs first. Once you do, you choose the technology that will best meet your needs, not the other way around.

Once you have a parent plan, you'll be able to bring technology into parenting in a way that will enhance and simplify—not complicate—your lives. It's all about understanding what your family needs and the workflow of your life, and then finding the technology that matches it.

I know that parenting isn't always easy, but I also know that it doesn't have to be overwhelming. For every family and every surprise along the way, there's a parent plan that will smooth the way and make the process an easier and happier one. When mistakes or surprises come your way (like they do with all of us), just make a new plan.

Beth Blecherman

1 | WHAT IS A PARENT PLAN?

It is difficult to plan for parenting, especially if you are a first-time parent who has never experienced the surprises and challenges of raising children. Even then, when you have another child, you may find that the way you parented your first child may not be well suited to another. Every child is different, every parent is different, and every family is different. However, if you have a process for parenting—a plan—you will find that parenting becomes easier.

In this book, you will learn about:

- the process of project planning
- how to create a flexible family organizational plan going forward
  - to identify your family's communication style and requirements
  - to create your Parent Plan, yearly, seasonally, and weekly

- o to develop time management, budgeting, purchasing, communication, and emergency plans.
- how to implement your parent plan

When you have a baby, you need to have a birth plan. Who will be in the room with you? Who will be your coach? Will you have natural childbirth? Maybe you prefer a midwife or want to film the birth. There are many choices, but one thing is clear—you need a plan. What's not clear, though, is what you'll need or have to do after your baby is born.

How are you going to raise this child? What will your family values be? What activities will your child be involved in, and what purchases will you make? How will you school your children, and what type of entertainment will be allowed? Like me, many parents wing these questions, scrambling to address each one as it arises, only to find that it doesn't work for everyone in the family.

A parent plan is the solution, providing the framework for a family, based on each member's individual needs, likes, and personality. Rather than only listening to others tell you what works best for them, you need to understand your own family and adapt your plan to it. Again, what works for one family, or even for one child, doesn't always work for others.

My parent plan doesn't tell you *what* to do, but *how* to do it.

As the parent of three boys, I've always enjoyed getting information from other parents, but rather than blindly following it, I use it as background to develop my own parenting style. For that reason, my parent plan doesn't tell you what to do, but rather how to do it. By providing the concept, I give you the groundwork to write a parent plan that works for your family, not the family next door. As I share the knowledge I've gained through years of consulting, project planning, and managing big projects, you'll learn how it use it in a way that will make your life, and the lives of your children, more organized and less overwhelming.

Like us, you will find that there are many parts of the parenting journey that may not be what you imagined, but if you keep planning (trying) toward your goals, you can reach them in one way or another. My husband and I conceived our first child the first time we tried and had our first son (a great surprise); we had five miscarriages after that (not such a great surprise). But we didn't give up—our plan was to have another child. So we added different options to our plan each time the current option did not work. Thinking about the next option helped me keep my emotions in check during a very difficult time. After lots of research, we tried a new version of IVF that gave us the gift of our twin boys. I have friends who also had trouble conceiving and have received the gift of a child or children, all using different plans.

No matter what journey you took to have a child, you are a parent. Regardless of the plan you used, you will face changes and surprises as your children grow through the years. Parenting is a moving target. With each stage of a child's life, there is something new to learn. Your child will respond to different experiences and situations as he or she matures and is exposed to different activities and people. As a parent, you have different things that make you happy, and you may be surprised to find that those things don't make your child happy—at all.

Parenting is a moving target with lots of surprises along the way.

While I did learn about child development "theory" by reading lots of books when I was pregnant, I hadn't learned some crucial skills that I would need every day. What's the one thing a pregnant woman needs to learn to do, more than anything else? They need to learn how to cook because that's one thing they will be doing for their families every day. I have three boys, and I'm cooking all the time, but I didn't learn the basics of cooking before I became a mother. Realizing that I lacked the necessary skills for something I was going to have to do every day, my husband and I made a plan. Before we knew it, we were not only cooking more, but our three boys were joining in the cooking fun, too.

Another parenting challenge that can benefit from a plan to learn more is the art of communication—not with adults, but with kids. I made a plan to improve communication with my kids. One of my lifesaving mommy books is by Kimberley Blaine, titled, *The Go-To Mom's Parents' Guide to Emotion Coaching Kids*. It provides the tools, tips, and solutions parents need to emotion-coach their child, as well as many real-life examples from Kimberley's own adventures in child rearing. She has taught me on several occasions that emotion-coached kids:

- relate well to their peers;
- play well with others; and
- move easily from group to group.

Ultimately, emotion coaching teaches children self-responsibility. This strategy is helpful because we all want our children to have a healthy dose of self-control over their lives at an early age so that, when they enter the challenging waters of adolescence, they won't go off the deep end. Kimberley reminds me that the developing teenager is similar to the budding preschooler—they're both looking for secure footing while experimenting with their newfound independence.

Just like other parents, we struggle to find the best remedies for the issues that challenge us in raising our own kids. I will forever be grateful for her book's core message: good parenting honors how children think and feel.

Good parenting honors how children think and feel.

In honoring how my kids think and feel, I made a plan to learn how they want me to communicate with them. From that plan, I realized my eldest son **would not tell me about his day** if I asked him **right after he came home from school**, but if we were **taking a walk or a bike or car ride together, then he would open up and talk to me**. Different children have different communication needs, so it is important to make a plan to understand and honor those needs.

Another example:

After years of watching one of my sons, John, become a passionate reader (and of history books, of all things), I was aware that his twin, Daniel, refused to read anything other than comic books. So I made a plan to help Daniel move down the reading path. The plan helped me determine that, while he needed support for reading, he enjoyed independently listening to books, so we bought him audio books he could read on our family tablets. Instead of refusing to read, he is now getting reading support and, at the same time, listening to books for hours each day.

These are things I certainly didn't anticipate. However, knowing each child and his needs helped me to address these situations and respond appropriately for him. Parenting has lots of surprises, but if you take time to plan, you can create a path to navigate your family life.

I've always liked being around people. When my first son was a baby, I took him to play dates and expected him to sit on the blanket, like all of the other kids, but he was always crawling off on his own into the far corners of the park. It was very distressing to me, and I kept trying to pull him back into the group. I didn't understand that being a parent means stepping back and understanding that my child is a person with his own needs and worries. Maybe I would have been more understanding instead of being frustrated that he wasn't engaging socially if I'd understood that the need to explore was part of his wiring.

You might be surprised to bring a child into this world and find that they are not like you. They may have different needs than you and, as a result, you need to be more than just understanding—you need to embrace their differences while helping them feel good about themselves as persons and helping them reach their personal goals in life. Because my son wanted to explore, but didn't like being confined to a group, I established a plan to find activities that we could both enjoy (such as hikes or bike rides). Your parent plan will have to include ways to do that.

You may find that your child changes over the years. For example, when your children become teenagers, they're going to become more independent, needing you less as they become more involved with friends and activities outside the home. I seek to help parents when these situations occur, so they aren't shocked or left feeling like they missed the boat.

Discuss safety and social networking *before* your child discovers Facebook.

Let's say you have a parent plan to start talking to your child about mature issues when they're ten, while they're still listening to you. Then, by the time they're thirteen, you've already been talking to them for three years, so when they start being affected and put weight on what their peers think, they will have your good parenting thoughts in their minds. Part of a parent plan means not waiting till your child is on Facebook to help him understand the rules of social networking safety—you should start at a younger age because by the time they're on Facebook, it's too late. I don't mean it's too late to have the discussion with them—it's just going to be a lot harder because they're going to be making mistakes before they know the possible consequences.

Another example of a time when it's helpful to plan ahead is in arranging summer activities for kids. Some people might not understand that, in many areas, in order to get your child into a summer camp, you have to start planning in January, especially if you are also coordinating schedules with your kid's friends. But what if a parent doesn't understand that and doesn't sign their child up until May? Their child may not get into the prime summer camps because they didn't understand the need to plan ahead. You need to sign your child up for summer camp in January or February, in the middle of winter.

Season passes purchased early can save money.

As a parent, you'll save both frustration and money if you plan ahead. By booking certain vacations early, you can save money. For example, when buying tickets for some amusement parks and sports activities, such as ski lift passes, you can buy a bargain season pass if you purchase it on a certain date before the season starts. One of my friends uses a plan of purchasing discounted ski lift passes for her whole family in April for the next year's ski season that begins in November. Some families learn the hard way. Because they don't plan ahead, they find themselves paying more or missing out entirely on some experiences. A parent plan would solve that, providing them with an instrument to follow from year to year that will prepare them in advance for upcoming events and life changes.

Creating a parent plan means looking ahead and understanding all the different phases of your life as a family member, as a parent, and breaking them into small pieces and tasks. It also means understanding the different phases your child is going through and talking to them long before they actually have that experience. For example, in regard to talking to your kids about the birds and the bees, you don't want to have that discussion when they're going off to college; you need to have it when they're much younger. Using a process where you think ahead, plan ahead, and start having these discussions years before they're actually going to be exposed to something will help prepare your kids for what's ahead.

Many parents are overwhelmed, especially first-time parents. They simply aren't handed the instruction book that tells them how to address each stage of their child's life. Conversely, if they were, that instruction book would relate to another parent's child, not theirs. That's why a parent plan is important. It provides each family with the framework to follow in the future, even if they don't know the skills they'll need or how to use them. As a parent, you take on different roles, including doctor, negotiator, cook, doctor, teacher, and if your child wants to play baseball, you may need to learn the game.

You have to be open-minded and realize there are a lot of new things that are going to come up and the only way you can handle this is to have a plan and try to prepare, and then revise that plan as life changes. Don't get upset, don't get frustrated, don't give up—just make a new plan.

Don't get upset, don't get frustrated, don't give up—just make a new plan.

This is one thing many parents overlook. It's more natural for people to know that they need a financial plan or a retirement plan, but what parents don't understand is that planning can help every part of their lives.

CHAPTER SUMMARY

The process of creating a parent project plan can mean the difference between being proactive (prepared) and reactive (unprepared). No fixed plan suits all families; this book instead shows you, step by step, how to create a plan tailored to your family's precise needs.

2 | FAMILY ASSESSMENT

2.1 | Family Assessment and Needs

The next step in project planning is assessments.

- What are the personalities and needs within your family?
- How do the different personality types interact?
- What individual goals does everyone in your family have?
- What barriers make it difficult to meet those goals?

As a parent, I believe you should conduct an assessment of your family to understand their needs, which will help provide input when creating family requirements. This information is important to understand before you make a plan to reach those goals (and overcome the barriers).

One child might be an introvert, while a sibling is an extrovert. One might be quiet and studious, while the other is rambunctious and athletic. As in relationships, parents can produce very different children.

Each family has different dynamics and needs. It is important to respect the various personality types because there are some things that people can change and some things they can't. For example, my husband does not like loud, crowded events, so understanding that personality type means that I will go to the events where there are loud crowds, and he doesn't have to, because I respect the fact that it makes him feel uncomfortable.

The process is basically about understanding what your family's personalities are and making your family work together as a team.

Example

Family Assessment

During the weekend, the boys need to attend events that include outdoor or indoor exercise, not only for health reasons but to help them sleep better at night. When they spend too much time indoors during the weekend, they become agitated and start picking fights with each other.

Plan

Help the boys find weekend exercise activities they each can enjoy, but that we can also do as a family.

2.2 | Family Communication

The next step in developing your parent plan is addressing family communication. What types of communication styles will fit those family needs? What type of communication plan can you set up to make sure your family is communicating the positive, the negative, the wants, and the needs of your family?

In many of my project as a consultant, we met to do a "brief/debrief" before and after meetings with clients. Before the meetings, we briefed everyone on what we needed to do to prepare for the client meeting. The debrief was when we discussed what happened at the meeting, confirmed the tasks that needed to take place, made sure we knew who was assigned to what tasks, and gave feedback on how we felt the meeting went.

The "brief/debrief" concept can be a valuable tool for families, as well as a way to make time to communicate when big events, milestones, or family issues come up.

Communication involves many different things.

- Is your family communicating with each other?
- How can you help your children communicate, both within the family and with their peers?

Establishing your family's communication plan will depend on your family's needs. This will vary over time, depending on the experiences your family members have, as well as your family's overall beliefs.

Families should also create communication plans to enable regular talks and feedback between parents and children. My own experience with family communication got off to a rocky start. Communication with my husband was easy, but, as a parent, I found it difficult to have "real" communication with my kids, that is, at first.

My first son's personality is the complete opposite of mine; his perfect environment as a child involved being outside with only a few friends around, so it was relatively quiet. I am very social and preferred to go to big, noisy social events because being isolated was difficult for me.

As I mentioned in the first chapter, during mother and baby playgroups at the park, I wanted him to hang out on the blanket with the other infants, where I could talk to other moms in a support group atmosphere. But, as soon as he could crawl, my son wanted to explore the park instead of hanging with the other babies!

During these outings, I was the mom hovering on the outskirts of the group, chasing after my crawling baby, instead of being with the other moms and their babies, where I could socialize and find support.

Luckily, family communication was in my plan, so we went to see a family therapist. She helped me realize that our personalities were different, which was causing us to clash, and that we needed one-on-one time to connect mom to son without outside stimuli. I was used to being around big groups of friends, so being in a one-on-one situation with my first son was an adjustment.

Making the change to being in quiet surroundings not only helped my son feel more comfortable, but it also helped us bond. I made a new plan to meet up with other moms when I had a babysitter or arrange small play dates with one other mom and her baby.

As my son got older, I kept exposing him to social events until I found ones that fit within his comfort zone. When he got older, he was able to communicate that there were some noisy social events that made him feel uncomfortable, while there were others (parties with his friends) that he enjoyed and he was at his happiest when in those situations. The key was always communicating to resolve the challenges of our varying family needs. Communicating your core beliefs should also be integrated into your parent plan, too.

Example

Communication Style

Our boys sometimes react to situations by wrestling and using other physical responses when their brothers are doing something to annoy them, instead of communicating with words.

Plan

Create a "talk time" during one meal per week where we discuss family issues. Then, discuss resolutions using words instead of wrestling.

Our talk times had different lengths and frequency depending on age. With my ten-year-olds, we had weekly talks and made a plan to use Internet safety controls to automatically filter out inappropriate material. When my older son signed on to social media at age thirteen, we chose to have daily talks with him. As I explained in several online articles, beyond the birds and bees, Internet safety is the new "talk." We set up a system of positive feedback when our son shared information about a about new online platform he tried that day and what happened.

As parents, we made a plan to spend the time and understand the privacy settings and safety issues of the online platforms our kids were engaged in and educate them on proper use. When our son presented a bad experience or mistake he made online, we helped create a plan to avoid it happening again. At the same time, he knew that the logical consequences of not sharing information about what he was doing online could include having his laptop or phone taken away. For our teen, we confirmed that talking about Internet safety while we were having a walk, driving in the car, or talking before bedtime was the most comfortable and effective time for him.

CHAPTER SUMMARY

The first step in creating a parent plan is to perform a family assessment in order to understand and clarify your family's personality types and communication styles.

3 | WHAT ARE YOUR FAMILY'S REQUIREMENTS?

Now that you have assessed your family personality and communication styles, the next step in a parent plan requires an understanding of what your family needs. As I've stated, what works for one family will not necessarily work for another. Each family will have its own unique requirements, based on the ages of its members, medical needs, educational goals, and the work, personal, and financial requirements of the family, as well as any extended family members.

3.1 | General Requirements per Age

What are your family requirements per age? Your family members will have individual and unique needs based on their ages. Of course, these needs will change throughout the years, which is why it is so important to review and revise your plan over time. For example, preschool, elementary school, middle school, high school, and college are all milestones that apply to your kids' ages, and each will have their own unique set of demands that need to be planned ahead of time.

Who is in your family and extended family? Your family may include parents who are living with you or will be living with you soon, so a part of your parent plan needs to address all of the family members that you'll be taking care of.

Example

Age Requirement

Preschool starts at age three.

Timing

Signups for our preferred preschool are open after our child is one year old.

Result

Sign up for preschool when my child turns one.

3.2 | Health, Nutrition, and Education Requirements

What are your family's current health and education requirements? These, too, will likely change over time, so your plan needs to be flexible and address your current needs, as well as potential future needs. It's all part of preparing and planning for both the short term and the long term. It is also important for family dynamics to understand the right learning environment for your kids. For example, one of our kids was not happy in his school environment, so we made a plan to find a learning environment that met his needs.

Depending on the medical requirements of your family, there are going to be health needs in the future, some of which you can anticipate and some which you may not be able to anticipate. This includes implementing preventative care that you can set up to help with your future medical needs. For example, how much sleep does everyone in the family need and how will you fit that into your daily schedule? Beyond the importance of naps in younger kids, I have found benefits in naps when I am not getting enough sleep at night. Another is that my family's history of cancer put me in the category of high risk. So, I determined the relevant cancer testing with a doctor and made a plan to take all the appropriate tests.

Families who think their child may have developmental or educational issues can set up a requirement in their plan to get an accurate diagnosis and, if necessary, implement a correlating support system at a young age. When we noticed one of our children reacted to loud group activities at his preschool by retreating to the back of the class, we made a plan to test him to see what was behind it. From working with professionals, we found out that our child's sensory makeup was sensitive to big crowds and loud noises. This information helped us make a plan with the teacher to adjust his activities to accommodate his sensory needs.

One of my friends had a second-grader who had trouble reading, so vision testing was one of the tests they conducted. He found out that his son's reading difficulties were associated with vision problems.

Your family's health requirements will include other activities that help your child develop physically, like dance classes or team sports. Exercise is a vital part of our well-being, for both parents and children. Ask yourself:

- How will your family get sufficient exercise?
- Will you take walks, hikes, or family bike rides?
- Will you join a club or gym?
- What about private lessons to help get started in a sport?

Some parents may prefer to test different sports to find one (or multiple) that their child enjoys, although preferences can change over time. I tried multiple sports with one of my kids until he found two he wanted to participate in: windsurfing and skateboarding. After one of my son's was bullied at school, we decided to sign up for a karate class that also taught self defense. Even though my sons were not going to use the karate skills at school, just knowing self defense made them feel empowered. If your kids have specific medical issues, then it is important to talk to their doctor to help you determine a sport that is appropriate for them. For instance, you may decide to pursue a sport like golf or swimming over sports that that are more physically demanding, such as soccer. Working parents may want to find an afterschool program that includes sports. Overall, it was beneficial for our kids to be exposed to different sports and then pick only the ones in which they *want* to participate.

If a parent enjoyed a particular sport when growing up, they may want to engage their kids in that sport in order to pass their knowledge on to them. For example, if you start jogging with your kids when they are young and they enjoy it, they may continue that sport into adulthood. We have a cousin who lives in New York City and runs marathons. He wanted to include his children in the sport, so he started by pushing them in a twins stroller during his runs. Then he took them to races featuring kid runs and found a local running program for kids. As a result, his middle-school kids are now hooked on running.

Some planning is like planting a seed—you plant the idea in your family and patiently wait for it to grow.

When my kids were young, we ran in a family race together, an event the whole family enjoyed. Looking back, if running was in our family plan, it would have been helpful to keep our kids engaged. Ultimately, we became too busy to run in family races and our boys lost interest. However, we keep running and offering opportunities for them to run. I call that "planting the seed."

We planted the seed in our boys that running was a good way to exercise by participating in the sport ourselves and regularly offering opportunities for them to run. While the idea did not grow into a sport that our kids wanted to participate in right away, they did when the timing was right for them. Looking back, it took about two years of patiently offering jogging opportunities to our sons before they decided to join in by training for a family 5K. While we have many tasks that are enforced (like homework), choosing ways to exercise and participate in a team sport were things we wanted our kids to decide for themselves (buy-in).

33

Some families prefer private lessons to help kids learn a sport. Whether it be hiring a neighborhood kid who is a few years ahead or finding a professional, there are many alternatives to fit different budgets. For example, some of the most effective baseball lessons for my younger boys were taught by a neighbor two years their senior. In my experience, finding someone who not only teaches sports strategies and techniques but is also a good personality fit with your kids is the best "lesson" plan for the family.

Fitting everything into a parent's busy schedule is not easy, but when exercise is one of the requirements in your plan, there is always a solution to any challenge. If you have a baby at home and don't have a sitter, you can use a stroller and go for a walk or run, join a health club with a good babysitting service, or exercise at home. I bought a jogging stroller for my twins and bouncy seats for them to play in while I used our home elliptical machine. To save money, I joined a local twins club with an online marketplace to purchase used twin-related exercise equipment (as well as furniture and clothes), instead of buying everything new. This extra step took some planning, but it saved significant money.

Part of the family's health requirements includes family nutritional needs. It is important to look at the nutritional and health needs of your family and see how you can support this with meal planning and the food you provide in your house. One of my friends wanted to teach her kids about healthy eating in a way that would not be construed as nagging, so she bought a book called *Red Light, Green Light, Eat Right* by Joanna Dolgoff, MD, to provide a visual way for her kids to learn about nutrition.

Families with allergies or medical issues may want to consult with their doctor or relevant specialists to create their nutrition plan. We have some mild allergies and a medical issue in our family, so we consulted with a nutritionist and several doctors to create our nutrition plan. Our nutrition plan requirements included finding a nutritionist who not only specializes in holistic nutrition but was also certified by the National Association of Nutrition Professionals.

Another of our nutrition requirements was to find healthy recipes for meals that are both easy and quick to make. So I searched through food blogs online and found many great recipe options. When I realized that part of my family nutrition plan to get healthy meals on the table included using a crockpot, I was delighted to find food blogs that were all about using crockpots, such as Stephanie O'Dea's blog, A Year of Slow Cooking (http://crockpot365. blogspot.com).

Lisa Stone, a friend and successful entrepreneur (one of the co-founders of BlogHer), shared her strategy of cutting, preparing, and stocking healthy food components, such as vegetables, beans, chicken, and salad, in the refrigerator so her teenage son could come home from high school and make himself a big salad instead of grabbing chips. I added "healthy food storage in fridge" to my family's nutrition requirements after seeing her fridge.

To engage our boys in cooking and eating healthy meals, we added a requirement to have them not only participate in cooking, but also in creating new recipes. We used the concept of cooking competitions to create our own family cook-offs. The theme of the cooking competition was "fun" and allowed each of our boys to use their own creativity in preparing a dish. We planned cooking tasks tailored to their ages. Our ten-year-olds cooked vegetables, side dishes, and desserts using fruit and vegetables as the main ingredients. We also allowed them to show their creativity in plating fish or meat dishes that had been prepared by Mom and Dad.

Example

Nutrition Requirement

Find a way for our family to eat more fresh fruit and vegetables.

Barrier

Not enough time to shop; fresh (preferably organic) food goes bad quickly if not eaten.

Budget

$40 per week, plus cost of new refrigerator storage containers (add to purchase plan).

Result

Find a local delivery service to deliver fresh fruit and vegetables once a week. Pick a service that offers a $40 mixed bundle weekly. Get a small compost bin to put in kitchen for fruit and vegetable leftovers and any that go bad. Create a system to wash, cut, or cook vegetables when they are delivered and store them in the refrigerator.

Your parent plan should also include educational goals. An education plan is very important, and it will change over time as your children age. What schools will be the best fit for your child's learning style? Are you going to send your kids to private school or public school? Are you going to homeschool? These are all things you need to plan in advance and your plan may include seeking a financial advisor who can help you budget in order to set up a college fund so you can afford to pay tuition when your child graduates from high school.

The parent plan may also include educational assessments if children have learning issues. There is a wide range of educational consultants or tutors that can be added to a plan if children need learning assistance. We made a plan to find a writing tutor to help our boys strengthen their writing skills before the upper elementary grades, where more writing is required.

3.3 | Personal Requirements

The next step in developing your parent plan is to determine the personal requirements of each member.

As a parent:

- What are your personal requirements?
- What are your exercise requirements?
- What are your personal time requirements?

Don't forget to include a social life in your plan. Do you or other members of your family have hobbies? What are they, and do they require any supplies, lessons, or costs that you need to include in your plan?

Parents need time alone with their spouse or partner. It's healthy for the relationship and makes them better parents. It's also true that single parents need to plan for time to date and develop relationships. This is important personal time to put into your schedule, into your parenting plan.

What are your requirements for "date night" with your partner, or what are your single-parent dating requirements?

Who will care for your children during that time?

As a parent, is there a way you can schedule some personal time, such as a night out with the guys or gals, every once in a while?

Parents need to plan for their own personal exercise time, too. I made a plan to determine my personal exercise needs, which helped me see that, because of my work and parenting schedule, I needed to find a way to exercise at home during the week and do family sports, hikes, or bike rides on weekends. Some of my friends enjoy exercising in the morning, so they go to a 6 a.m. class and are back in time to get the kids off to school before they go to work.

Another area you need to consider in your plan is finding clothes that fit your budget and lifestyle, make you feel good, and are flexible to the busy schedule of a parent.

Example

Personal Requirement

Fit exercise into daily work and parenting schedule.

Plan

Switch lunch dates with friends to walking lunch breaks, take family walks or hikes, buy a used exercise machine for the garage, and join a health club to have an exercise plan designed. (Add both to budget and purchase plan.) Schedule workouts on calendar to make sure not to miss them.

3.4 | Work/Financial Requirements

Ask yourself:

- What are your career and work plans?
- What are your partner's career plans?
- What is your plan for establishing work/life balance with your kids?
- What are your requirements for house and childcare?

If one partner or spouse is going to stay at home, how does your financial plan compensate for that? If both partners/spouses are working, what is your financial plan for childcare? What key requirements per age of your family members, e.g., savings, college, vacation, home purchase, private school, braces, remodeling, are going to need financial investments?

The work and financial requirements of families are very diverse, depending on their income, housing, health, long-term goals, and the number of people in the family. There are many variables. For instance, if one parent or partner will stay home with the children for a period of time, they may need to invest in training to stay current in their field to prepare to return to work in the future. My mother was a single parent, but she found a way to save enough money for us to go to brunch and get tickets to a matinee theatre performance a few times a year—that was a special treat that my brother and I will never forget.

If one parent has a personal dream of transitioning to a startup and becoming self-employed or going back to school for job training, then that too needs to be addressed in the financial/work requirements for your parent plan.

My Story

After I had my twins, I identified a career transition requirement in my plan to make sure I kept my job skills up to date and to prepare me for work. So, in 2003, I got on the web to look for parenting support, and that's when I witnessed the early start of online blogging.

By 2005, I was ready to start my own blog, TechMamas.com, that I developed while co-founding the Silicon Valley Moms Group (hyper-local mom blogs across the country), which we sold to Technorati a few years later.

I decided to build my brand online around my website, TechMamas.com, so I started sharing (or curating) information on families and technology on various social media platforms, including Twitter®, Facebook®, YouTube®, Google+® and Pinterest®. Social media offers anyone the ability to create an online brand to share their voice.

My work requirement was to define my niche (family technology) and regularly update my social network platforms to create an online brand I could use to get a job when I was ready. Many parents have built their brands online by using blogs and social network platforms, but those who make careers out of it have a business to back up the brand.

Having an online brand can benefit anyone with a business—for example, a baker who creates cakes can gain exposure by sharing details of their cake designs using social media. Many participate in social media to reach out to an online community, like the professional community on LinkedIn®, while others enjoy it as a hobby. Some jobs, like doctors or accountants, require licenses be kept up to date. Even parents who want to get new jobs, additional training, or transfer into a new industry can benefit from a plan. That plan helped me get job opportunities when I was ready to start working again.

A parent plan means you need to plan for work/life balance. Your job will have a major impact on work/life balance. Some families switch, changing which parent will work and which one will stay home with the children, depending on job availability.

Having childcare is perfectly fine, but having the right childcare is a very important requirement for families.

- Will you hire a nanny or use an in-house daycare provider?
- What before- and after-school accommodations will you need to make for your children?
- What transportation will be necessary to make it work?

If either parent's career plan includes working at home, other requirements might include extra space at home for a home office. You may have to pile your kids up in one room to make space for an office. Maybe part of your career requirements is finding a workspace outside the home. I identified that requirement, so our parent plan included joining a specific health club because it had a business office where I could work when necessary.

If both parents want to work and hire an *au pair* as a sitter, then there needs to be an extra room for him or her. One of my friends planned for her *au pair* by buying a house that had a big basement, which gave them extra room to build another bedroom. When it came time to hire an *au pair*, they converted part of the basement to a private room. Another friend's kids shared a room so there would be a room available for her *au pair*.

Other parents I know who either worked out of the house or at home in their offices used various types of sitters, including afterschool programs, nannies, nanny sharing, afternoon sitters, and even night sitters to solve childcare requirements.

What are the financial implications of one parent/partner staying or working at home? This also requires a financial plan because there are a lot of write-offs. You may need the advice of an accountant who can help you plan for the tax implications in the future. Be prepared by setting it up in advance.

Don't forget to include financial investments, savings, and retirement requirements in your financial plan. This is one area you should review annually to determine whether you're on track; if not, you can make adjustments as necessary to make sure you are. As your income changes, so too will your financial responsibilities and needs. With each change comes an opportunity to update your parent plan to prepare for the future.

Hiring a financial advisor or accountant can be an essential requirement for a parent plan. There are many online websites that offer financial advice, financial planning tools, and apps. You may include finding the right personal, family, or business lawyer to your plan. This is another resource that is important to plan in advance, before any true emergencies arise. The lawyer might support personal legal issues, such as a will, as well as other professional legal issues, like reviewing work contracts. It is important to spend sufficient time finding the right lawyer, especially if you are starting your own business.

Planning ahead for how you are going to monetize your service or business by setting up the proper legal and accounting structures is an important step to do—sooner, rather than later.

Example

Parent Plan Requirement

Update Mom's career skills.

Timing

One year—the youngest will be in preschool, and there will be more time available to work.

Plan

Identify skills needed to transition to new career, take night/weekend classes or find an online class (add to budget plan). Join LinkedIn.com (business networking site) and try to connect with those in your new industry and arrange informational interviews to identify skills needed for your new career.

3.5 | Resourcing Requirements (a.k.a the Art of Delegation)

Childcare, household assistance, tutors, and professional advisors are to parenting what resource planning is to managing projects. Resource planning means that you need to look at the resources needed throughout a project and then make sure you have assigned the appropriate person to fill that need, either within the organization or by hiring outside help.

That's just one instance. There are many other ways parents can use the concept of resource requirements. For example, defining what chores need to get done in the house and assigning specific chores to every family member old enough to help is an important part of the family resource plan. We waited too long before we attempted to assign chores because we assumed mom and dad would get many of them done much more quickly. In the end, that left mom and dad spending too much time on chores, at which point I recalled how my single mom raised me not only to help around the house, but also to help care for my younger brother.

That's when we decided to assign household chores to our three boys. After we saw the boys not only doing chores, but also feeling proud of their hard work, we wondered why we'd waited. Who knew that one of my twin boys loved to wash the car and help cook dinner, or that my other twin son wanted to vacuum or empty out the dishwasher? Best yet, my teen son could fold and put away his own laundry.

After we saw the boys not only doing chores but also feeling proud of their hard work, we wondered why we waited so long to ask them.

To make developing the chore list a family activity, we allow the kids to pick which chores they want to do from the list (buy-in). This includes alternating among siblings, if some chores are more (or less) popular than others.

Another example is related to my own business. I spent years attempting to create my own graphics and headshots for my website. While doing my personal resource requirements, I realized that spending hours trying to do this took valuable time away from my parenting duties and work projects. I concluded that graphics design and photography are not my strong points. This helped me see that one requirement should be to delegate those responsibilities, similar to assigning tasks to specialists when I was managing my project plan. So I invested in professional photos (www.babyjidesign.com) and the services of a graphic designer (www.xfactordesigns.com). Having professionals handle my photos and graphics was a great investment and helped me take my business to the next level.

Next, I admitted that I would likely never get this book written without finding and hiring some resources to help me through the book-writing and publishing process, so I hired Alicia Dunams (www.bestsellerinaweekend.com) to help me move forward.

I met other social media entrepreneurs like myself through social media platforms such as Twitter and social media conferences such as BlogHer and shared ideas with them to understand other resourcing options available. Kimberley Clayton Blaine from TheGoToMom.TV offered great examples of resource requirements, such as hiring an assistant to help enter the details of all of the business connections she makes from attending conferences and that come in via email to a database she can use for business outreach. By not resourcing the assistance I needed in organizing my business contacts from my email and conferences, I was missing out on paid jobs because I didn't have the bandwidth to return all the emails.

Another resourcing issue was choosing professional clothes for my post-baby shape. Even though my youngest kids were now ten, I had a different body shape than before kids. An assessment of my clothes helped me grasp that I was still buying clothes fit for my shape before I became a mom. I was also shopping online to get deals, viewing the clothes on models. My clothes shopping process left me with a closet full of stylish clothes that did not fit my shape.

This clothes assessment helped me establish a requirement to delegate by hiring a stylist to assess my closet (and me) and pick out new clothes that complemented my post-baby figure. She not only helped me get rid of what did not fit, but also organized them into bags that I took to a (high traffic) consignment shop. To my surprise, the shop not only took 75 percent of the clothes I brought in, but, if they all sold, I would make enough money to buy new outfits. My new plan included shopping with her a few times a year (during sales) to stock my closet for different business occasions with items that actually fit. The new style plan would be to have fewer, higher quality clothes that actually fit.

Delegation as a parent doesn't only mean delegating work to have more time to parent. In addition to having kids help with household tasks, it also means that some families may need to hire help, if it fits within their budget plans.

Keep in mind, hiring someone to help clean your house once a week may be an expense, but view it using the basics of accounting. If it leaves you with more time for work to bring in income, or if it will offer you that precious "more time with the kids," which can be considered "love" income, then it should be added to the plan. One of my mom friends shared her favorite "resource" hire to keep household tasks in check when she went back to work: she hired someone once a week to fold laundry and clean the house. She told me this still left plenty of chores for her kids to do.

Last, when it comes to helping your kids with homework in subjects where you don't have expertise, defining resource requirements can help. Is there a local kid who is a few grades ahead whom you can hire as a homework helper? Or, if your child is falling behind in a subject, is it a worthy investment to add a tutor to your home resource plan? Your family will get a return on its investment as your child strengthens his skills in the subject.

I suggest to single men and women that their requirements include finding a partner with compatible ideas about what their parenting role will be; or, if you find out your parenting ideas are not compatible, make a plan to compensate so that everyone's needs can be met. I have friends whose spouses/partners travel often. Because they are able to do so, they hire full-time help. It's a plan that works for them. On the other hand, I have friends who enjoy being the primary parent because they get to set the rules of the house and develop a routine that works, almost like being a single parent when their husbands are traveling.

There is no one secret to achieving the ideal work/life balance.

Friends who are single parents have used resourcing strategies, such as babysitting co-ops or hiring a sitter who does household duties, as well, including grocery shopping. The biggest fallacy is that there is one secret to work/life balance. My friends and I like to quote something that has been said by many before: "Once you accept there is no true work/life balance, then you just enjoy your parenting journey." Or, as a mom of three boys, my plan is to just "embrace chaos!"

Because I was not bringing in a full-time income after I left my consulting job, I experimented with after-school programs and hired help after dinner, when my husband was home. This plan allowed me to go to evening events or work, while the sitter and my husband put the kids to bed. I always made sure to kiss my boys goodnight and cuddle with them when I was working at home.

Working at home and managing the kids, however, is a challenge I still struggle with today. If I had my family project plan from the start, I would have evaluated our childcare options in advance and been ready to act. Instead, I found myself reactive to the changing nature of parenting three kids.

One of the items I wish I had done differently was not waiting to do our remodel and instead going ahead right after it was approved. The remodel would have given me the option (and room in our house) to hire an *au pair*, which, in the end, is the only true full-time childcare that our family could have afforded. Instead, over the years, we had a potpourri of different sitters, after-school programs, and carpool shares, none of which gave me the full freedom to go back to work full-time. My requirement to find the right childcare was something I found hard to implement.

When my youngest children were in kindergarten, I finally found a strategy that gave me a flexible work schedule: a fabulous after-school program that picked up the kids and went until 5 p.m. (and was a supportive and fun learning environment that my boys loved). There are multiple sitter strategies that may work for each family. For our family of three boys, we found that sitters (male and female) who had a sports interest worked best because they engaged the kids in sports and helped them stay active. The more sitter options, the better!

The upside to using after-school programs or group childcare as a requirement is that they save money. The downside is that if your child is sick or there is a school holiday, the parent in charge of daily care of the kids will need to stay home with them. Some of my friends used the strategy of hiring full-time help to account for the irregular school schedules and after-school activities. During the day, they had their full-time help do the shopping or other errands for the house.

Many of my friends switched the parent (or partner) in charge of the kids during the day, depending on which parent had the best job opportunity. As I mentioned before, my mom was a single parent, and we lived in an apartment, where other families shared in helping to walk the kids home from school, so maybe I learned from my early experiences.

Overall, many single and working parents seek jobs that have some flexibility as a way to deal with the unknown surprises of parenthood. One of my single working friends used the creative strategy of forming carpools and support groups with other parents who could help in childcare emergencies.

I started to identify my career requirements when my kids were babies. My career transition plan was very helpful in identifying the need to build my personal website and brand, while working at home until my family situation changed, and then looking for work outside the house. (One of those steps led me to writing this book.)

I have friends in many different situations—full-time working parents, stay-at-home parents, and work-at-home parents—all with differing childcare situations. Among them, those who had their own versions of a family project plan seemed to be better able to adjust to the dynamic nature of their family situations. Watching the different requirements and strategies other parents used—some that worked and some that did not—helped me determine my own strategy/family project plan.

Another example of delegation is carpooling or finding a sitter to meet a weekly need. We have a family requirement for our twin elementary school sons to play baseball, because they love it and we want them to play at least one sport. My requirement is to take my boys to baseball practice each week, but my barrier is that sometimes I have meetings that overlap practice, or I have to drop my older son off at an event elsewhere. I needed to delegate driving my boys to practice on some days.

Example

Resource Requirement

Help with carpooling to baseball practice.

Plan

Look into carpooling with other families ($0) or finding an afternoon sitter who drives ($15–30 per hour). If we need to hire an afternoon sitter, we add that cost to our budget plan.

In a perfect world, I would be able to set up a carpool for driving with the other families on the team and only have to schedule meetings on the days I am not driving. But when you are a parent of twins in a world with smaller cars, sometimes it is hard to find another family (or families) to carpool that has room for two kids plus their own and other kids. I asked another mom how she handled her child's sport schedule while she was working, and she explained that she found an afternoon sitter who could drive.

Because a regular sitter was not in our budget, I worked out a system with my husband for him to leave work early to take our twin boys to practice on the days I had meetings. He told me he wanted to be at practices anyway, so my having identified a need to delegate a task ended up being better for everyone involved. I have seen all sorts of carpooling used by single parents, working parents, or parents double- or triple-booked with activities who need help. Carpooling does not always require the well-known minivan; there can be biking, walking, or public transportation pools.

3.6 | Family and Vacation Time Requirements

- What are your family time requirements?
- How are you going to juggle a busy schedule with spending quality time together?
- What are your family vacation requirements for the year? What is your kid's vacation schedule from school? Will you be sending them to camp, "staycation," or vacation during school breaks? For camps or vacations, when are the timeframes to receive discounts or use air miles to fly?
- Do you want to have one evening in a week where you are together?
- How do you want to spend time during the weekend together?
- What are your vacation family time requirements?

After family and vacation requirements are defined, the next step is to decide how to include flexibility into the plan. For example, what family time can slide a little bit when life gets busy? What kind of family time do you want every week or every month to make sure you have time together, no matter what? Maybe Friday or Sunday night is for a family dinner (no tech allowed). Or perhaps more family dinners can be squeezed into your plan. You need to decide this ahead of time because life will move very fast, and if you don't have a plan, you will miss out on regular family time. Another strategy is to have the whole family attend their siblings' weekend sport events as family time.

Other family-time strategies that act as double duty for family chores are shopping together at the local farmers market and then cooking together, or cooking together after weekend religious events, going to family races, or even working on a household project together.

Some of the most memorable family-time events for us have been when we help cook Thanksgiving dinner for a local shelter. Volunteering in the community is not only a great family-time event, but also an opportunity to demonstrate to kids the importance of giving back.

How are you going to juggle a busy schedule so you can spend quality time together? This includes vacations. What types of vacations do you want to take? Vacations take time, money, and planning to select places and activities that are suitable for kids of different ages. The school year is a busy time for many families, so planning for vacations with the goal of spending time together and relaxing is important.

Should your family vacation requirements include active vacations that involve traveling to different locations or ones that settle in to one location, such as renting a house at the beach? Alternatively, your vacation requirement may be to choose a location that has events for the kids separately (to have adult time)—or do you want to do everything as a family? For those families that want to stay local, what seasonal local events or attractions can be included in your vacation requirements?

Your family time requirements will change over time. When your children get closer to being teens, they're not going to want to be around you all of the time, so these are things you need to plan in advance in order to take advantage of the time you do have together as a family. While my teen would now rather spend the afternoon skateboarding with his friends, he still enjoys a family day together watching a baseball game or spending a day at the beach. So, we adjust the family activity requirements to the interests and ages of our kids.

Preschool to Elementary School-Age Vacation Time

Our strategy was to find family-friendly vacation locations, such as Disneyland and other theme parks, beaches, parks, camping, exploratory museums, aquariums, and any resort with a kids club. Matinee performances for music or theater top off vacations with kids. But the best resource for family-friendly vacations is the network of parent travel blogs that cover locations around the world! Most of all, the money-saving strategy of a "staycation" can still offer lots of fun activities for families. The parent travel blogs suggest local events that can make any resident feel like they are on vacation. Every time we spend the day at a nearby beach, we feel like we have been on vacation.

Vacation Time in the Teen Years

Vacations with teens are tricky, but, at the same time, there are more alternatives for vacations with older kids. I recommend checking out parenting travel blogs to get ideas to create your family requirements for traveling with teens. When we go on vacation, we make sure there is an outdoor or sports activity component that will make all three of our boys happy, or we go to a location that offers different experiences for different ages.

For example, when I took my tween on a Disney® press trip on the Disney Dream® Cruise Ship, he was excited to visit a club on the boat designed exclusively for teens. This gave him a chance to hang out with other kids his age, while I had the chance to visit the champagne bar to have a drink with another mom.

Example

Summer Vacation Requirement

Find day camps and activities for my ten-year-old twins.

Timing

Signups open in January; be ready to book by then. Vacation house rentals also book up by early spring.

Budget

$4,200 for the summer or $200 per week, per child, for 10 weeks of day camp.

Plan

Could not find camp for $200; found great camp for $400 per child; signed up for two weeks for each child ($1,600). Rented a beach house for two weeks ($2,400) and made play dates and day trips for other weeks ($200), totaling $4,200.

3.7 | Bucket List Requirements

- What is your bucket list of things you want to do and places you want to go?
- What are your family's bucket lists?
- Which ones are you going to plan for and how?

Life goes by quickly, and suddenly we find ourselves in the future we always talked about, but never fully prepared for.

- What are your dreams?
- What are the things you truly want to accomplish during this lifetime?
- How can you plan ahead of time to make them happen?

That's your bucket list, and it's a very important part of your parent plan. Don't wait until the kids are in college and say, "Hey, wait, we never did this!" or, "We never did that!"

For example, when Kimberley Clayton Blaine asked me to go to the fabulous Paws Up Ranch in Montana to shoot an episode of MommytoMommy.TV, I said yes, not only because I enjoy appearing on MommytoMommy.TV, but also because the location on that particular ranch was on our bucket list. I had to evaluate this because I would be paying for any of my expenses that weren't covered and related to the video shoot. While it would be a big investment of our own money, it was on our bucket list, so we decided to do it.

Example

Bucket List Requirement

Vacation on a ranch with activities for kids, including learning how to ride horses, in big mountain country with open ranges to go horseback riding.

Timing

Signups are open one year in advance. Book at least nine months in advance to make sure there is space.

Budget

Found ranch in Montana that is normally out of our price range. Add vacation cost and any clothing needed for the kids to the budget plan.

Plan

Book vacation at ranch one year in advance. Start extra savings fund to save for trip.

There are many people, books, and websites that give advice, but I've found that most of them focus on providing solutions. While there is nothing wrong with solutions, a solution is only good if you know the problem and if it is the right solution for you and your family. To find the unique solutions for your own family, you need to step back and understand your own requirements. Then, turn to friends, family, relevant books, blogs, websites, apps, or other resources for examples of strategies and plans for ideas. Next, take your family's requirements and tailor a plan that helps you find solutions.

3.8 | Planning for the Unexpected

As I have explained with the other requirements, setting up a plan means that you need to look ahead at your family's goals and break them down into tasks (buckets). However, unexpected events, such as divorce, death of a family member, sickness, job loss, or other serious incidents, can necessitate a major change in the family plan. Other types of unexpected events, such as a child who excels in a sport to the point of training to become an Olympic athletic, can result in demands that can cause a major change in the family plan as well.

As parents, we try our best to provide what we think is the best education for our kids, but, in an unexpected twist, we may find out that our choice is not the right learning environment for our child. In that case, it is important to revise your plan by looking at your child's new requirements to see if your current educational solution can still accommodate your child's learning needs. This may be extremely overwhelming, especially if it means changing learning environments to find one that works.

While my son scored at the advanced level in testing, he was not a good fit for the local middle school that he and our family enjoyed. We set our personal emotions aside to take the time to understand our child's new requirements, and then made a new plan. That path led us to a new school for creative kids that offered a more ideal learning environment for him.

We have talked to parents who used other resourceful solutions to find the right learning environments for their kids, including switching public schools, homeschooling, charter schools, all types of private schools, or signing them up for learning academies that offer one-on-one instruction.

Education is another area supported by great online resources for parents and a strong community of email lists and social networks where families can meet others with the same educational needs.

The teenage years can surprise parents by changing the child they once knew into a teen with new emotions and issues. I have had comical debates among my friends on when exactly the teenage years start. Some feel that they start at the end of elementary school, not to mention middle school! The changes brought by the teen years might be anticipated or completely unexpected; regardless, they will probably require you to make revisions to some part of your plan.

The act of creating a new plan can also help you to refocus during a time of emotional stress. Some of the bravest parents I know have dealt with mental or medical illness by letting themselves feel the emotion, and then moving on to making a plan.

These extreme situations are another great reason to reach out to the online community, at first maybe to read about other parents going through the same challenge or perhaps to share your story online to gain support. I've found that the beauty of parenting websites and blogs is that, no matter what happens in my life, there is always someone else (if not many others) who has had a similar experience, so I don't feel so alone. In fact, while I get wonderful support from my local friends, there are some issues that I like to keep private, so reading online parenting articles and posts helps fill that void.

There are many parenting email lists that are good places to find other parents going through comparable challenges, both positive and negative. This is an area that will inevitably change with the flow of technology—for example, while some still use parenting email lists, others use private groups within social networking sites.

One of my friends found out that her child, who was in elementary school, needed to be on a virtually gluten-free diet. She joined a local email list of gluten-free families and reads gluten-free food blogs and websites. Another mom and dad I know were determined to put a plan together to try whatever treatments it took when they found out their teenage daughter had cancer. They updated family on her status on a website for families dealing with sickness, which allowed them to set up a private group for family and friends.

Some of the bravest parents I know have dealt with their own sickness while raising kids, which not only changed the type of family plan they had, but also changed their perspective on life: *to allow themselves to feel their own emotions about the sickness, while trying to achieve as many special moments with their kids as they can.* They embraced the help of others, too, even allowing websites to be set up so that friends could sign up for meal deliveries.

Another thing that is difficult to plan for is depression. Some struggle with it their whole lives, while others experience serious bouts of depression as parents. Jenny Lawson has a site called The Bloggess (thebloggess.com), where she has eloquently articulated depression in numerous posts. Many people have commented on her posts, expressing not only their support, but sharing their own struggles with depression. It is this type of interaction that highlights the power of online communities and social media. While you can't plan for depression, you can plan to get help, if needed.

When unexpected challenges come up in your life, getting input from others in the same situation can help provide background for you to revise your existing plan. When we had my first child, we joined a newborn hospital group that met once a week. Meeting up with other parents of newborns was not only a great source of support, but also humor. We all joked as to whether we had showered since our last meeting the week before.

Another thing to plan for in the age of technology is backup and recovery. Every important item that your family has stored on their computers or online should be regularly backed up. What if your computer crashes and you don't have an up-to-date backup drive or use a backup service? What if you use an online calendaring system and it goes down? Do you have a backup calendar? Even important paper documents should be part of a backup and recovery strategy. For example, is there an important photo album that you should scan a copy of and store in a safe place?

Example

Planning for the Unexpected Requirement

 To have a backup of important family documents and memories in case of a disaster.

Plan

Create a backup and recovery plan that includes storing documents in the cloud, choosing "auto-load" for pictures on smartphones to the cloud so pictures will be available even if the phone is lost, performing full backups of family computers to backup hard drives, and storing select important documents in a safety deposit box.

CHAPTER SUMMARY

Identifying and developing a list of your family's requirements is critical to any parent plan. This includes requirements dictated by age, health and nutrition, education, personal, work/financial, resourcing (hiring) needs, family time, your bucket list, and planning for the unexpected.

4 | DEVELOP A PARENT PLAN

Now that you've established your family requirements, you're ready to develop a parent plan to help you keep your family organized and prepared for the future. The information you've identified so far will help you create the appropriate steps or tasks as you plan for key milestones and events in your life, and ensure that you are prepared to fulfill the requirements of your family. A quote that is used by many applies to how you should look at your parent plan—as a *journey* and not a *destination*.

Your parent plan is a journey, not a destination.

4.1 | Overview: Develop Your Core Plan

The first step in creating your family plan is to take the requirements you put together and start converting them into either one central plan or mini-projects, both of which need assigned tasks and timing (dates). Some families will prefer to have one central plan with many tasks, while others may feel overwhelmed by this approach and want to start with a main list and then create mini-project plans.

To understand the steps needed to create your plan, here is a diagram you can use to help get the process going.

---

1. Define Family Requirement:

What is your family requirement?

2. Barriers & Buy-In:

Is there a barrier you must overcome to fulfill this requirement? What will ensure buy-in from the family?

3. Define Steps (buckets of time):

Define the steps and deliverables of your plan.

4. Documentation:

How are you going to document and have family "check in" for your plan?

5. Additions to Purchase Plan? What Is Your Budget?

Define what to add to your purchase plan and budget.

6. Revision Needed?

Decide whether your plan is working; if not, revise and redefine new steps and deadlines, if relevant.

↓

7. Positive Confirmation
or Logical Consequence:

Congratulate yourself and your family—for either reaching goals or trying their best! They've earned a hug, reward, or logical consequence (per family rules). Always give hugs, no matter what—positive reinforcement!

Details of the Parent Plan Overview

1. Family Requirement

- What is the family requirement?

This is the step where you take either one or multiple family requirements to build into a plan.

2. Barriers and Buy-In:

- Is there a barrier you need to overcome to fulfill this requirement?
- What will ensure buy-in from the family?

This is the step where you need to identify either any barriers you have had in the past or ones that may come up. That will give you the chance to plan for what you need to overcome those barriers.

It is important to identify what you need for those family members who need to participate in that task to buy in. Without buy-in, it is hard to carry out tasks. The buy-in may be connected to a logical consequence for the kids, but the best buy-in from family members happens with positive reinforcement.

3. *Steps*

- Define the steps (tasks) and deliverables of your plan.

By breaking up each step and assigning tasks to those steps, you will be able to turn your plan into a reality. Tasks that are overwhelming can be broken up into smaller steps, mini-projects or phases (Phase I, Phase II...). Some steps may need to be prioritized into high, medium, or low for creating the timeline to complete each task.

4. *Documentation*

- How are you going to document and have family "check in" for your plan?

When you implement that plan, there is a step to create the documentation. However, it is best to plan for what type of documentation works best for your family so you are ready to implement your plan.

For example, some may want to use whiteboards and others spreadsheets or planning software, while some may just want to create a list, and then update their family schedule with the tasks. Everyone has their own comfort level when it comes to documentation. The key part of documentation is having a way to assign dates, note who is assigned what task, and fill in the task status or check when it is done.

This is the part of the plan where technology should be considered as a good way to automate plan documentation. For example, using online calendars can be a great source of organizing tasks and reminders (such as a reminder to sign up for summer camp when signups first open).

5. Additions to Purchase Plan? What Is Your Budget?

- Define what you need to add to your purchase plan and budget.

Once you create your plan details, you may find you need to purchase something to support a step. It is important to plan for that and, of course, make sure you have the budget for the purchase. If not, this is the time to create a savings plan and put in your current plan any stopgap solutions for what you can do until that time.

For example, while we needed a new refrigerator to have more space to carry out our family requirement to have healthy, cut-up food ready for the kids to eat, we can't afford one just yet. Instead, I have put in my plan that we need to reorganize our current refrigerator.

Revision Needed?

- Decide whether your plan is working. If not, revise and redefine new steps and deadlines, if relevant. If the steps seem overwhelming, this is the time to break up the steps into smaller steps, mini-projects or different phases (Phase I, Phase II, etc.).

This is the time to check with your family (and yourself) whether the plan is realistic and working. For example, in my exercise plan, I decided to go for a run three times a week. While I kept to that plan for weeks, I became aware that not only did I not look forward to my runs, but they were not giving me the results I wanted.

I revised my plan to incorporate Pilates group classes (when I had time), walk with friends once a week, and go back to doing my abdominal exercises while watching TV at night and working out on the elliptical machine, either at home or at my health club, depending on what fit into my parenting and work schedules. While my friends were getting in great shape by running weekly, because I did not like running, it did not work for me. Instead, I found exercises I enjoyed more, which was much better for my plan.

Positive Confirmation or Logical Consequence

- Congratulate yourself and your family—for either reaching goals or trying their best! They have earned a hug, reward, or logical consequence (per family rules).

Always give hugs, no matter what—positive reinforcement inspires family members to keep reaching for their goals. But, in some cases, logical consequences may need to be implemented instead.

For example, my teen enjoys playing videogames with his friends as a way to relax after school. We have a family rule that homework and exercise need to be done before he sits down to play videogames. There have been times when we needed to use the logical consequence of either shutting down the gaming console or even taking the videogame disk into our room, with the rule that it could only be used with permission. This consequence worked to remind our teen that gaming screen time needs to be earned and will be taken away if he does not comply with the family rules.

We found, however, that the key to our parent plan was a lot of positive reinforcement when our kids met their goals or finished tasks. A hug and encouraging words from parents to their kids go a long way toward building their self-esteem and helping them become responsible. The best-case scenario is that your children not only learn while watching their parents create a plan, but that they take responsibility to start creating their own plans, too.

4.2 | Develop Your Plan by Year, Season, and Week

Develop a Yearly Plan

The next step is to review your plan to include yearly tasks, events, and/or milestones, and then add/change your core plan accordingly. What are the different stages that need to be planned for your family per year and per age? To do this, you'll need to look at the different ages of your family and start to plan for what you're going to need for those different stages.

Maybe your child needs to go to preschool, public school, private school, or be homeschooled. If so, start listing your options to determine how you will make that happen.

- What type of school and after-school activities will you need to plan for?

- If your child will be homeschooled, will you be the person doing the homeschooling or do you want to take them to homeschool academies that provide individualized education?

- If your child has learning issues or special needs, what education plan will be best for them? Do they need to have any evaluations that year?

- Do you need to plan for a school change the next year (such as going into high school)? If so, what can be planned in advance?

Yearly plans will be impacted by medical or dental events, such as planning when a child will get braces or when specific doctor appointments or medical procedures will be needed. Yearly planning can ensure that parents don't miss the opportunity to prepare their kids for events, such as allergy season, by scheduling their visit to the allergist and developing a plan for allergy medicine or allergy shots.

Preschool yearly planning is not only important in finding a preschool, daycare, or activities at home, but in starting the process to expose children to different sports and physical activities, such as dance or gymnastics, to see which ones they like (which will, of course, change over time). Without a plan, it may not be clear that soccer, baseball, and other leagues start in kindergarten, so it is good to start soccer classes or play before they are in kindergarten.

When we had our twin boys, we decided we needed a plan when it came to sports. Before we signed them up for soccer and baseball, we attended some local sports classes with the kids to learn basic rules before they started the leagues. Another option is to create a plan to practice a sport at home, maybe even buying simple equipment (such as a soccer ball or baseball pitch back net). Or plan to hire a neighborhood kid who is already active in that sport to help kids learn the rules. Don't forget, though, that sports are important for girls and boys alike; some of the best soccer players we know are girls!

Lesson Learned

We made a plan to help our kids not only find a sport they liked, but give them opportunities to learn the basics of the sport in other ways, rather than just being in sports leagues. Looking back, my oldest son wished he had stayed with soccer, but, at twelve, he found it too late to step back in. Our plan to keep exposing him to sports until he found one he liked worked: he took up windsurfing and skateboarding. In the end, every child can find their path to a sport if there is a family plan to find one they like.

If you need to work, yearly childcare requirements may need to be identified. From ages one to six, you may opt to have them in a preschool that goes till five o'clock, but, when they're in elementary school, you may decide you're going to need to hire a nanny.

If you need to hire a nanny, you have more considerations. Is it cheaper to hire an *au pair* (who usually works on a yearly rotation)? If an *au pair* is part of your plan, it is important to plan to have space in your home to accommodate them.

Do you need to find other families to carpool with during the school year? If so, it will be important to find other families in similar situations that are involved in similar activities. For example, some families may want to carpool with others that have a flexible schedule, so if there is an emergency, someone else in the group can switch slots.

It takes a village.

The saying, "It takes a village," applies to parenting, so it is important to reach out to a local circle of friends, if needed. Beyond carpools, I have even seen families do cooking rotations, where one family cooks extra food and shares it with other families so they can get a night out (to share a meal with other families).

Example

Yearly Plan Step

Create a yearly, school-based family calendar that can be updated and shared with all family members.

Timing

In September, after school starts.

Plan

Collect all school and extracurricular activity calendars to create family calendar. Update the calendar on the family computer, then make sure it can be shared with all family members via online calendars and related mobile apps.

Develop Your Seasonal Plan

The next step is to review your parent plan for seasonal events and update it as needed. Ask yourself: What are the seasonal needs of my family? Every family goes through different seasons, and the school year is one example. Summer is a season. For those who live in really cold areas, winter is a big season that they need to plan for; so the seasonal needs of your family are an important part of your parent plan. Holidays also require special considerations.

For instance, during the summer, you may need to find activities, play dates or hire more help because the kids are not in school. Planning for summer camp, as we discussed in the first chapter, typically needs to start in January in order to find the best camp for your child and ensure there is an opening. Or maybe you look at your financial plan and realize that summer camp for all of your kids is more expensive than the family vacation you have all dreamed about, so instead of signing up for camp, you plan a summer vacation or rent a summer house.

That's why seasonal planning has to happen at the same time as you're doing your yearly plan. If, during the requirements phase, you decided that you only need help during the school season, then you can prepare for the school season by hiring help in advance.

Seasonal planning should take into account school breaks.

Seasonal planning should take into account school breaks, too. For example:

- When do your kids have a break from school?
- What activities will you plan for them?
- Will you:
  - go on a family vacation?
  - sign them up for camps?

- o coordinate with other moms for play date house swaps?
- o go on local outings?
- o hire childcare if you work?

Many schools have minimum days and school holidays that will require planning ahead. Websites, blogs, and online communities that offer local activities for kids are great resources for school break ideas. Homeschooling online groups, websites, and blogs offer ideas for educational and local entertainment options for kids and families.

Example Family Requirement:

Parent Plan for Seasonal School Breaks

Requirements: Identify seasonal breaks, potential activities for the kids, and budget.

Timing: September or as soon as we get yearly school schedules.

1. Identify **Thanksgiving, winter, summer, and other school year break schedules.** Determine if kids will be at home, camp, or involved in family travel. Determine deadlines to book camps and family travel accommodations.

2. Compare school break schedule to work schedule and determine whether we need to **hire a sitter or get help from family or friends.**

3. Identify potential activities depending on season, including ski trips, local day trips, play dates, events at local health or sports clubs, visits to theme parks, family travel, day camps, overnight camps, specialty camps (such as digital media camp for those kids wanting to learn more about digital media). Other activities include camps that allow kids to participate in volunteer activities or internships for high school-aged kids.

Create school break activity plan, including purchase plan.

Determine overall **family breaks budget,** including accessories needed (for example, if we go skiing, we need to buy ski clothes for the kids; for camping, they may need camping clothes or accessories). Identify whether there are any pre-season sales for vacation travel packages or accessories. Determine early bird savings for break camps.

Then make a plan!

After you develop your seasonal plan, the next step is to consider a weekly family plan.

Develop a Weekly Plan

Every family has a flow, and that includes weekly tasks. Weekly includes things that happen each week, so what can you do to plan for those things?

For instance, let's look at cooking. Maybe you cook on Sundays for the whole week in order to save yourself time during the week. In that case, you'll have to develop a menu plan and a corresponding shopping list for your meals during the week. Or, if weekly shopping is an issue, planning to shop online for grocery or local organic stores or use food delivery services that can save time and enable you to do more cooking at home. If there is a night when cooking is not an option, plan for a weekly night out at a restaurant, but choose one that is convenient and budget friendly, according to your family's needs.

One of my weekly requirements, again, was for my family to eat more fruits and vegetables. My mom friends and I always say, "Your responsibility is to put healthy food on table, whether they eat it or not." But I really wanted my boys to actually eat more fruits and veggies, so I made a plan. This plan included any barriers that had previously prevented me from accomplishing this task.

Family Requirement:

To eat more fresh, local fruits and vegetables.

Barriers:

It is hard to find time to shop, and fresh fruit and veggies go bad if not quickly eaten.

Parent Plan for Fruits and Vegetables:

Buying:

I can sign up for a local organic fruit and veggie delivery service, supplement with one trip to the store each week, and set up planter(s) to grow some at home.

Cooking:

Involve the kids in picking out recipes they like with fruits and veggies, and cook for multiple nights when delivery comes. Find kitchen gadgets to help when cooking with a busy schedule.

Reuse:

Make soup or cooked dishes with fruits and veggies that get soft if we don't use them quickly. Compost scraps and those that go bad.

Add to Purchase Plan:

Already have crockpot; will need to buy small compost bin and sign up for delivery service.

Last year, the stress of cooking on the nights my twins had Little League was overwhelming so, on those days, we found a local wholesome restaurant where we stopped to eat on the way home or I planned to have a meal ready in the crockpot. Planning weekly meals during Little League nights released so much of my stress and made baseball season far more enjoyable. This example also highlights how some family events are seasonal.

Another good example of what to include in a weekly plan is a chore list. Here is an example of how to develop your parent plan for delegating family chores:

Example Family Requirement:

Assign Chores to Kids

Parent Plan for Family Chores:

Requirements: Teach responsibility and get help with laundry, dishes, and cleaning. (*It is exhausting for mom and dad to keep up.*)

1. Have family meeting to discuss which chores each child would prefer to do.

2. Decide when the chores will be done.

3. Define how chores will be documented and the logical consequences if they are not done.

Create Daily Chore Plan:

1. Basic chores: clear dishes from table and load in dishwasher; put dirty clothes in hamper—floor does NOT = hamper! Put away folded, clean clothes in closet.

2. John will take out trash.

3. Megan will load dishes in dishwasher.

4. Joe will vacuum or wipe floor.

5. Weekly chore list will be created as a digital file, printed each week, and posted in the kitchen. Kids will

check off list after chore is done. If chores are not done, allowance will be deducted.

6. If an increase in allowance is needed, folding laundry or doing other household chores will earn extra allowance.

Added to Purchase Plan:

Wet mop that is easy for Joe to use.

4.3 | Time Management Plan

One of the biggest challenges of being a parent is time management. Some of the basic concepts of project planning help you break up projects into smaller tasks (or buckets), but even more important than planning for daily tasks is managing your time. This concept can be very helpful in your parent plan. I like to think of it as breaking up your day into buckets that offer flexibility.

Every day, parents need to do many tasks at different times, some separate and some that require multi-tasking (accomplishing several tasks at the same time). If you have something that is not getting done: Some tasks have timing considerations so priority levels (high, medium, low, for example) should be considered to help with timing. Key questions for time management include:

- Can you slip it into a different time bucket?
- Is there a barrier that you need to work out?
- What tasks are time dependent?

- What priority (high, medium, and low) should each task be assigned?

For example, we found that we had no problem fitting in washing clothes, but then we were left with piles of clean clothes lined up in baskets, waiting to be folded. I evaluated whether this was something we could fit into the "chore" bucket for the kids and timing options, such as folding laundry while watching TV (multi-tasking). I looked at each part of my day and identified where I could fit extra tasks into that time bucket.

Small things like this can be great timesavers, even if it means saving time by wearing your workout clothes to bed so you can get up extra early one morning to work out before the kids get up—*not that I ever do that...*

As a work-at-home parent, I realized that my best hours (sweet spot) to get work done are from 9 a.m. to 2 p.m., so I try to fit my work into the morning timeframe bucket and move shopping and errands into other buckets, like after I drop the kids off at their after-school activities or at night, when my husband is home.

When my kids were little and went to bed at 8 p.m., I was able to put some extra work into my "second-shift" bucket after the kids went to sleep. But, when my kids got older and did not go to sleep until after 9 p.m. (needing more attention at night, such as reading stories, etc.), my second shift disappeared. This made it even more important to fit my work into my 9 a.m. to 2 p.m. "sweet-spot" timeframe. In fact, I found I was three times more productive working during my sweet-spot work time than when I was when trying to do work at 10 o'clock at night.

While I best empower my day by exercising in the mornings, that is also the best time for me to work, so I either fit in a quick workout in the morning bucket or take walks with my family after dinner. I have workout equipment and videogames (especially dance-themed) that I use to sneak in a quick workout if I have extra time buckets available throughout my day. Sometimes I fit exercise into my social time bucket by taking a walk with a friend, instead of sitting down for coffee.

When I transitioned back into working full time, I evaluated options such as hiring a sitter during the day and moving household tasks to nights and weekends. For example, I considered different ways to fit in exercise throughout the day while working at an office, such as walking up and down the stairs at lunch. Fitness experts, websites, and tools (like those that count steps or apps that track how far you have run) can be very helpful in creating a fitness plan that fits into the time buckets you have each day.

As always, with parenting, you need to be flexible because there will be days that you have planned out perfectly, and then one of your kids gets sick and you need to stop and take care of them. In that case, you rearrange your daily tasks into different time buckets and focus on taking care of your little one. Another option is to arrange emergency care or have a spouse or family member help out, if needed (part of your childcare planning).

Creating a time management plan will allow you to identify tasks, consider timing issues (barriers) related to those tasks, and then assign tasks into different time buckets. Rearranging tasks into different time buckets gives you the flexibility to switch the timing around until you find the one that fits. Then, when timing changes, like it always does with family activities, you just rearrange the time buckets to create a new schedule.

Rearranging tasks into different time "buckets" gives you the flexibility to switch the timing around until you find one that fits.

Example

Time Management Plan

Mom's Work (at Home) Daily Time Management Plan	Time
Morning:	
Work during sweet spot (Mom's most alert)	9–2 pm
Exercise during lunch break	1 hour
School pickup	3 pm
Carpool to sports and lessons	3–6 pm
Grocery shopping and household errands between carpool stops	1 hour
Homework	7–9 pm
Email, light work tasks (Mom is too tired to do heavy-thinking work tasks) and household work	9–11 pm
TIME SHIFT: *During full-time workweek: Find a sitter or other parent to drive carpool; grocery shop at night or weekends. Exercise in morning before kids go to school.*	

4.4 | Develop Your Budgeting Plan

An important part of a parent plan is defining your family budget. What is your:

- weekly budgeting plan?
- monthly budgeting plan?
- annual budgeting plan?

Knowing and preparing a family budget plan ahead of time will help you make sure there are no surprises and that you are financially prepared to meet your family's needs.

You need to make sure that you either have the money to pay for each requirement in your plan or prioritize and cut some requirements from your plan. Having a budget means you can say, "It's going to cost 'X' amount and my income cannot accommodate it, so I'm going to need to make some deletions or revisions to my plan." For instance, by budgeting, I discovered I would not be able to hire as much outside help as I needed.

- What future financial goals do you need to put in place to meet your family budget needs (budgeting/financial plan)?

- What resources do you need to hire to help with your budgeting plan (accountant, financial planner)?

Financial planning is one of the most important areas to get help, if it's needed. Not only are there are many types of financial advisors, but there are also websites, blogs, and apps that offer financial advice and tools. Don't wait until your child is entering high school to save for college—but if you do, still make a plan to make it happen.

Example

Budgeting Plan

Summer Budget Item	Cost	Amount taken from monthly budget	Amount needed to save in summer account
John:			
Baseball summer camp (1st two weeks of August)	$200 per week	$400	$400
Megan:			
Digital photography camp (1st week of August)	$300	$300	$300
Joe:			
Baseball summer camp (1st two weeks of August)	$200 per week	$400	$400
Family:			
Trip to visit New York City relatives	5 plane tickets— use mileage points	0	0
Meals and activities	$500	$400	$400
Total		$1500	$1500

4.5 | Develop Your Purchasing Plan

A purchase plan is made up of the items your family will need to purchase as defined by your requirements. What do you need to purchase for your family on a daily, weekly, monthly, or annual basis? This includes clothing, food, school supplies, bedding, medicine, furniture, toys, books, activities, presents, TVs, computers, phones, and possibly automobiles.

After you have a plan that identifies your needs, drawn up a budget, and decided what you're going to buy, then you decide when and where you're going to purchase it. What are you going to buy? If it's a TV for watching movies on family nights and you know this ahead of time, you can start looking for sales to find the best price.

A good example is if you're buying a bedroom set for a ten-year-old boy whom you know is growing. Will buying a twin bed be sufficient, or, in three years when he's thirteen and has had a fast growth spurt, will his feet be hanging over the edge? In that case (as was true in my personal experience), it might be better when he's ten to purchase an extra-long bed, rather than a standard twin.

Here's another example. One of my friends was having trouble deciding what type of TV to buy. I suggested that, if buying new, she might as well invest in an Internet-enabled TV, which would allow her not only to access media from her cable provider, but also from the Internet (which at the time was the most current feature available). It was the perfect solution for her family. When I purchase a new laptop, I always buy one with the most up-to-date features so it will last longer.

Another friend did not want to buy a new TV but still wanted Internet access on his, so I suggested he add an Internet-enabled set top box to his purchasing plan, which would add Internet connectivity to his existing TV.

Yet another friend simply wanted to watch movies in her backyard. I suggested she include adding to her purchasing plan a mobile projector that connects to her tablet or computer and use a white sheet or big outdoor movie screen to project it.

Sale websites and blogs that discuss ways families can save money are good ways to find information to support your purchasing decisions. There are many online shopping sites for families, such as CoolMomPicks.com and CoolMomTech.com, which offer reviews from a parenting perspective.

Example

Purchasing Plan: Computer and Workspace

Family Computer Workspace Purchase Plan	Cost	Amount taken from monthly budget	Amount needed to save in summer account
Equipment:			
New laptop	$700		$700
External monitor (for larger viewing screen)	$200		$200
Printer	$100		$100
Computer desk	$300		$300
Chair	$100		$100
Mouse pad	$10		$10
Paper for printer	$10	$10	
Ink refills	$80	$80	
External wireless keyboard and mouse	$100		$100
Total		$90	$1500

4.6 | Develop Your Communication Plan

Part of your parent plan is converting your communication assessment and requirements into your communication plan.

Now that you know everyone in your family has varying communication needs, how will you bring it to together to communicate as a family?

Once a month, will you get together and talk about things that are going on in the family and have everyone give their feedback on what needs to be changed or what can be improved?

Will you do that during your Friday night dinners?

How are you going to establish regular communication?

How will you get your spouse or partner and children to buy in and actively participate?

There's more to it than that—part of the communication plan is how you are going to change. Once you've identified that there is a problem, how are you going to resolve it? Everyone needs to be open to hearing feedback.

Example

Communication Plan

Family Communication Plan:

Create Family Rules:

What are the rules we will use to respect and communicate with each other?

Create Weekly Time for Family Check-In

Weekly Communication Activities

What times or activities during the week to use for Family Check-In (family dinner, walk)

Topics for Weekly Family Check-In:

What is working in your family communication, and what is not? What happened that was good and what happened that was bad that week? Each family member also shares one thing that each family member did or said that they liked and one they did not like and how it can be improved.

Special Family Check-In Events:

What special events can be used to help bring family closer through quality family time?

4.7 | Develop Your Emergency Plan

Nobody likes to think about them, but emergencies happen. Some are avoidable, while others are not, but pretending they won't occur can leave you unprepared and throw your lives into chaos. What types of emergencies should you plan for? What is your plan to deal with emergencies?

Emergencies can constitute the potential for severe weather or similar events, such as an earthquake. If so, buy earthquake supplies and show your kids where they are and, if necessary, how to use them. Your emergency plan should tell your kids what to do and where to meet in the event of an earthquake. The same is true of tornadoes and hurricanes. Many families have fire safety and evacuation plans.

Once you've identified potential emergencies, look for resources that will help you prepare for them. For instance, if you live in California, source websites that cover earthquake preparedness. You might find online courses in first aid that your family can take, or you might want to register your child for a child safety/stranger danger class in your area. Teach your child how to use a cell phone and make sure they know emergency contact numbers so they can use any phone to get help.

Family illnesses are emergencies. You may need to teach your children what to do in the event there is a fall or injury. According to the age and health of your family members, your emergency plan should be personalized to it.

Another emergency to prepare for is computer failure, as mentioned at the end of chapter three. While a computer disaster may not be as urgent as a natural disaster, families keep important information in digital format, so regular backups is an important task to include in your plan.

The last step is creating a backup and recovery plan for your family's important digital and paper files. In this step, it is important to identify all of the important files and paper documents and then create a plan for how you will not only backup (and recover), but also how often you will need to refresh your backup plan with new information. Family insurance is an important item to consider in emergency planning.

Example

Emergency Plan

Example Emergency Plan: Earthquake Preparedness	Date Done	Expiration Date
Supplies:		
Buy earthquake food and supplies Create schedule to rotate and update items after expiration dates		
Buy utility supplies (flashlights, batteries, radio, bottled water, blankets, clothing)		
Create family emergency communication plan (where to meet, who to call) Create copies to put in kids' backpacks		
Create list of house maintenance items & instructions (e.g., shut off gas; activate backup generator)		
Update kids on location of earthquake supplies		

4.8 | Develop Your Personal Needs Plan

The last step in creating your family plan is reviewing it to make sure family needs and personal time are included. This is the time to go back to family members to see what their personal time needs are. For example, my kids like to have at least one day a week after school where no activities are planned and they can just relax—their personal time.

Many parents feel isolated because they do not have much free time. It is important that plans are designed to help those who feel isolated get the connections they need. For example, if you are home at night after the kids are in bed and are interested in social media, that may be a good time to write blog posts or connect with people on Facebook, Twitter, Google+, or other social networking platforms. There are many online communities for parents that offer support and advice.

Another important part of your personal needs plan is making time not only to spend with your family, but also out with friends, social networking, both online (such as LinkedIn or Meetup.com) and live events, such as local parenting groups, sports, such as running clubs, hobby groups, such as book clubs, and professional networking groups. It is good, too, for parents to see whether they can get childcare and go away for a few days, whether with their spouse, partner, friends, or—my personal favorite—social media conferences.

One of my preferred social media meet-ups is a conference called BlogHer. I went to my first one in 2006 and made some of my favorite social media connections through those live conferences. Of course, sometimes getting childcare just to sit at a café and read a book now and then can be a great addition to any personal time plan. One of my favorite spots to write this book was at a local café that not only served great food, but my favorite teas (and a whole section of artisan chocolates!).

Example

Personal Needs Plan

Personal Needs Plan:

Make plans with other families or adult friends; attend business networking events

Make a List of People and Organizations to Connect with

Decide on Activities to Do with Friends:

Girls' or guys' night out, invite families over for dinner, sign up for a professional conference, join a local hobby or sports club

Choose Dates and Update Calendar:

Sign up for events and clubs; send out emails to friends to choose dates

Resourcing:

For events when sitter is needed, check that one is available; if not, hire a new one or talk to families about babysitting co-ops; check to see whether family or friends can help cover childcare for girls' or guys' night out

Budget and Purchase Plan:

Decide on purchases needed for events (e.g., new running shoes for running club, new dining table that fits more guests, new professional outfits), and update purchase plan; check budget plan for what can be purchased now, what needs to be saved for, and what can be purchased on sale or used

4.9 | Develop Your Technology and Workspace Plan

Once you've determined those specific needs, ask yourself how technology can help you with your plan. As a technologist who covers family consumer electronics online, I know how valuable a tool technology can be for families. At the same time, I recommend that families determine their requirements before making technology purchases. The biggest mistake is to make purchases based solely on price, availability, or what's popular without determining your family's specific requirements.

To do this, review all of your requirements, then decide where technology can be added to the plan to assist with those requirements. For example, let's use a requirement that many families need: taking and storing photos. Listed on the next page is a diagram that shows the process of moving from identifying requirements to a solution you can plan for.

Example

Technology Plan

Family Requirement:

Organize Taking, Storing, and Sharing Family Pictures

Process

Take pictures at home or on the go, store them, then share with family; note: for some situations, there is water involved and outdoor conditions

Can tech assist with taking pictures?

Taking Pictures

Use my smartphone to take spontaneous pictures on the go, coupled with a thin, light, waterproof point-and-shoot digital camera (also used for outdoor conditions)

Storing Pictures:

Store on PC and cloud: set phone to instantly upload pictures to cloud services, or use camera with wireless transfer to mobile device to upload to the cloud.

Sharing Pictures:

Give family access to photo albums on cloud storage site or load photos and print photo albums using sites such as Shutterfly or Snapfish

Add to Purchase Plan:

Already own smartphone; need to purchase digital camera.

When creating a plan, keep an eye out for new technology that may solve that need. For example, while looking at photo storage alternatives, I discovered online services that enable the ability to import photos from your computer, phone, camera, and online social networking websites, to be stored, viewed, and shared from one location.

Another example is buying a computer. Before buying a family computer, you need to determine what you will be using the computer for:

- work
- homework
- media consumption (watching movies, listening to music)
- content creation (websites, photos, video)
- light family tasks (displaying calendars, digital photos, recipes, slideshows)

Tablets, smartphones, and computers can stream all types of media, so options are plentiful. For homework or general work, computers are the best fit. Full-size keyboards are the most comfortable to use for long periods of time, but wireless keyboards can be used to extend functionality for mobile devices.

If the computer is shared between family members and needs to stay in an open area for parents to monitor, then a desktop is typically ideal, but a laptop connected to a bigger external screen can also fit the same needs. If the computer needs to be mobile, there are many options, including laptops or tablets that come with different form factors. Technology websites and blogs offer buying guides and reviews that can help provide background when making technology decisions.

For kids, it is important to understand their technology requirements for schoolwork.

- Can they use the family computer, or do they need their own device?
- If for school, do they need a tablet for:
  - online research?
  - reading eBooks?
  - educational apps?
- Do they need their own laptop for word processing, spreadsheets, presentations, or other content creation?

Families wanting a device that does not tempt their kids with apps yet offers the ability to read digital books should look at eReaders, although some eReaders have tablet features, so the lines between these are blurred—some eReaders have tablet functionality, while many eReader apps are available on tablets.

There are many types of assistive technology that can help students with learning differences, such as voice dictation software and apps, smart pens that convert writing and voice during class to electronic format, smart keyboards for those who need to type instead of writing, websites such as Audible.com that offer audiobooks, and software programs to help with learning and school organization.

If a child has a learning issue, parents should investigate and then input into their plan the use of various assistive technology offerings. It's even better if they can coordinate with their kid's school to bring assistive technology into their child's classroom when needed.

Before kids are allowed to surf the web or use apps, they need to understand web safety. Some families may want to install web filters or set up safe search and video sites to make sure they are not exposed to inappropriate sites or material. Because technology is available at many places that kids visit (other homes, schools, libraries, etc.), the top requirement for all kids should be an education on web safety and etiquette.

Luckily, there are many websites that can help parents and kids learn about web safety and etiquette, including CommonSenseMedia.org and the Entertainment Software Rating Board (ESRB.org), which provides ratings for computer and videogames. For example, parents should develop family rules on technology and educate their kids about why web safety and etiquette are important and the possible consequences.

In an article at *Laptop Magazine*, I explained that web safety is the new sex talk, which expresses not only how dangerous being online is, but also how important it is that parents have the web safety talk to educate their kids.

At some time, your child is going to want a phone. People come to me, through my website and in person, asking me to help them understand what that entails or develop a plan for implementing a phone for their kids.

Cellphones and smartphones are a technology requirement for many families. For a child's first phone, I usually recommend a low-cost one (with an inexpensive plan) that has a keyboard, but does not have any Internet access.

The right time to start considering giving a phone to your kids is when they become more independent and are going to school or afterschool activities on their own. Getting their first phone is an opportunity for children to demonstrate their ability to be responsible enough to have a phone, so a basic phone that only allows calls, or perhaps texts, is appropriate.

As kids get older and demonstrate more responsibility (usually around the teenage years), their social life will move to mobile devices for texting and social networking—and they will probably ask to upgrade to a smartphone with a data plan that allows web browsing. Our teen had a small phone with a keyboard and no Internet access for two years, until he was twelve. By then, he had shown he was responsible with the phone, so we allowed him to upgrade to a smartphone.

Budget considerations include a child's ability to stick to a certain amount of texts, phone calls, or data usage. Overages can be a very expensive lesson if controls are not put in place to cut off the account after the limit has been reached.

Communicate regularly with kids on web safety and social networking etiquette.

Before teens join in online or social networking via apps, they need to have a solid education on social networking etiquette and web safety. For example, I told my son about the importance of respectful electronic communications, and the consequences if he didn't communicate with respect. This includes discussing not only what cyber-bullying is, but also how to respond if he sees someone else getting bullied online.

For any kids who have cameras on their phones, the talk needs to include understanding what is appropriate to photograph or video and what is not—and, again, the consequences for inappropriate behavior. I tell my teen to make every social media update or electronic communication appropriate enough that even a future employer or college recruiter could see it. It is important to have regular communications with kids about web safety and social networking etiquette.

Part of the technology plan needs to include family technology rules, such as what types of technology are acceptable per age, screen time limits, and a parent's favorite: how kids earn their screen time. Technology is a powerful tool, but it also can be powerfully addictive for children of all ages. The journey of learning to balance the power of technology with limits is a lesson that needs to start at home. Screen time has limits and is earned in our house.

In my article on Technology Consequences at the website Mashable, I shared that, once family technology rules are set, they need to be enforced in order for kids to respect them. Our sons earn their screen time, which covers all screens, including TV, computers, and tablets, by doing chores and homework. One of my friends drove across country during the summer with her boys and required six pages of work from math and English workbooks to earn screen time each day. The consequences my family uses include losing screen time and, in some circumstances, taking technology away.

For example, if our teen does not get ready for school in the morning because he is distracted by his phone, we not only take the phone away until he is ready to go to school, but we bring the phone into our bedroom that night as well and do not give it to him in the morning until he is ready for school. If our elementary school twins don't turn off their screens after their allotted time, we shut them off and don't allow any screen time for the rest of the day.

Once families decide on their technology requirements and develop a plan to educate their kids on web safety and social networking etiquette, they can decide on a budget and then choose the appropriate electronic device or accessories.

For example, let's say you're spending $50 to go to the movies. Maybe you can purchase some home technologies so you can have a home theatre, which may be a little bit of an upfront investment, but, since movie night is in your own living room where you can provide your own snacks and won't need transportation, you'll be saving money in the long run. There are other ways a technology plan can help a family save money. Instead of getting a tutor and paying $35 an hour, maybe there's an online class available or one of the many free educational websites (such as the Khan Academy) your child can source. If so, the purchase of a computer that your child can use, both now and in the future, might be a good investment that will save money in the long run, as well.

Another area to plan for is an organized workspace in the home for your family. The Resources Section at the end of this book will direct you to more information on organizational resources.

CHAPTER SUMMARY

Developing your parent plan includes developing a plan by year, by season, and by week. Additionally, plans for time management, budgeting, purchasing, communication, emergencies, personal needs, and technology/workspace should be created.

5 | IMPLEMENT YOUR PARENT PLAN

Congratulations! It took some time, but you've finally completed your parent plan. Rest assured, subsequent plans will take far less time because earlier versions will be used as the foundation for the next year's plan.

5.1 | Create Planning Documentation

A plan isn't a plan unless it's documented. Therefore, it is beneficial to put your plan in digital format, where you and your children can update it on a regular basis. Which form of planning documentation works best for compiling your parent plan and sharing it with your family?

Everyone has their own documentation style. I like lists, spreadsheets, and flowcharts, while others may prefer checklists or full-fledged, detailed plans. Sometimes, part of the plan may be putting the plan on hold in order to deal with a big project or family issue.

To write this book, I had "drop everything days," when I did not worry about any of the household duties, work that did not have pressing deadlines, or other non-urgent tasks in order to make time to write. To create time to write my book about project planning, I had to put other parts of my plan on hold. The beautiful decorations surrounding me while I wrote included piles of clean, unfolded laundry in baskets, a refrigerator lacking its usual healthy fresh foods, and house projects half done.

Usually, I would have re-delegated household duties so that my family took on more, but they were equally busy with their own projects. I learned to tell myself that the plan was to ignore any non-urgent tasks until I finished my writing.

Some people are overwhelmed with plans. In that case, they can check their plan and then put it away, checking it again when needed to make sure they are on track. Others may want to document and display the plan and check it daily.

The ultimate goal of your parent plan is to provide you more quality family time.

Most important is that your plan serves to guide you to get things done, without preventing you from enjoying and engaging with your family. Before I started making my parenting plan, I felt like I was distracted whenever I spent time my kids because of all the tasks swimming around in my head. After I made my plan, I could put all thoughts of my tasks aside and freely engage with my kids. When you look back, it is the quality time your family spends together that is most important.

How can technology be used to help with your parent planning process and make it more efficient, not only for you, but also for your children? Do you want to start by writing it, then converting it into a digital format? What digital format do you want to use: software, such as Microsoft® Office, cloud-based tools, or project planning software or apps?

If you run a business, you can use project planning software, such as Basecamp®, contact management software, such as Constant Contact®, accounting software, such as Quicken®, or you can use one of the selections of apps that perform mobile project planning tasks. For more information about project planning tools, please check the Resources Section, which will direct you to updated information.

Do you want to record a family brainstorming session and then convert it to a digital format afterwards? For free-flowing creation of requirements or plans in a flowchart format, I like to use Microsoft® PowerPoint.

Example Family Requirement: Assign Chores to Kids

Parent Plan for Family Chores:

Requirements: Teach responsibility and get help with laundry, dishes, and cleaning (*it is exhausting for mom and dad to keep up*).

1. Have family meeting to discuss which chores each child would prefer to do.

2. Decide when the chores will be done.

3. Define how chores will be documented and the logical consequences if they are not done.

Create Daily Chore Plan:

1. Basic chores: Clear dishes from table and load in dishwasher; put dirty clothes in hamper (floor does NOT = hamper); put away folded clean clothes in closet.

2. John will take out trash.

3. Megan will load dishes in dishwasher.

4. Joe will vacuum or wipe floor.

5. Weekly chore list will be created as digital file, printed each week, and put in kitchen; kids will check off list after chore is done; if chores are not done, allowance will be deducted.

6. If an increase in allowance is needed, folding laundry or doing other household chores will earn extra allowance.

Added to Purchase Plan:

Wet mop that is easy for Joe to use

When I make my plans, I like to use a spreadsheet to set up the task list for my family to follow, like the one shown on the following page.

CHORE	Who	Mo	Tu	W	Th	Fri	Sat	Sun
Basic Chores: clear dishes from table; put dirty clothes in hamper; put away folded clean clothes in closet	John							
Take out trash	John							
Basic Chores: clear dishes from table; put dirty clothes in hamper; put away folded clean clothes in closet	Megan							
Load dishwasher	Megan							
Basic Chores: clear dishes from table; put dirty clothes in hamper; put away folded clean clothes in closet	Joe							
Vacuum or wipe floor	Joe							

For example, maybe you can create a family calendar online that everyone can see and update. There are many apps and websites that offer calendar and planning tools for families. There are many other tools that assist with organizing and finding information online. While I like to create my parent planning documentation on my laptop, using my ergonomic full-size wireless keyboard and mouse, there are document, spreadsheet, and presentation software that are cloud-(online) and app-based, for use on mobile devices, such as tablets and smartphones.

At this time, you'll be implementing all portions of your parent plan, including the financial planning sections. You should be actively referring to your plan to determine what you need to do and when you need to do it to ensure that you are able to fulfill the requirements of your plan.

If you know you won't be able to implement a portion of your plan for a particular reason, such as not having sufficient funds, you may need to hire outside help to create financial and budget plans.

Because this is a plan, it's about looking ahead, always staying one step ahead of the curve, and knowing what's beyond it. Refer to your plan regularly to determine what you need to purchase, what milestones are approaching in your lives, and how those things will impact your finances and the other aspects of your plan.

Once you create a parent plan, you then need to set aside time to look at it regularly, updating it to accommodate miscellaneous and life changes, and to address feedback. You may have received feedback that Friday is not a good night for your family to get together for family time, so maybe you'll change it to Sunday night.

Flexibility and the ability to adapt to change are important. Because of that, it is important to prioritize what parts of your plans are high, medium, and low priorities. The high priority tasks within your parent plan should be given priority if your family situation changes, while the lower priority tasks can be changed, re-categorized, or deleted to adapt to family changes.

For instance, you might have a requirement that family night is on Wednesdays, but, when your son entered high school, you found that he has team practice every Monday and Wednesday evening. In this case, if it's important that the entire family is together for every family night, you'll want to change family night accordingly right away, instead of waiting until the end of the month.

Another example is when the family member who is tasked with the chore of folding clothes gets very busy on a big project and does not have time. Maybe that would be a good time to support them and share that task between family members. You need to be flexible. Most important, as a busy parent, you need to be flexible with yourself.

While I schedule my shopping tasks to be done after my work day is finished, there are just some days when I need to go food shopping in the morning. To make sure my visit is efficient and brief, I make a shopping list beforehand and, when packing up the groceries, I make sure all the cold items are grouped together. This allows me to come home, quickly put away just the cold groceries, and get back to work. At night after my work is done and the kids are in bed, I put away the non-perishable groceries.

My favorite example of being flexible, though, is giving yourself the flexibility to know that you can't do it all. Some of my mom friends are forever stressed that their houses are not always neat. I like to say that it is important to spend time creating an organizational system that everyone can use in the house, but, at the same time, realize that, while it is important to clean your house, keeping a perfectly neat house (including my house of three active boys) is something that's just gotta give! So if you make a plan that is not fitting with your work life balance, then make a new plan.

When you make a plan, sometimes you need to take baby steps to implement it.

Along with being flexible in changing the plan, another technique is to either implement the plan by taking "baby steps" or just implement parts of the plan so you don't overwhelm yourself or your family. For example, because of medical issues, we had to change our family diet based mainly on protein, vegetables, and fruits, with small amounts of healthy carbs. Reworking the family diet was overwhelming at first, so I took baby steps by first making a plan to reorganize our shelves, then reorganize the refrigerator, then work on finding recipes and creating shopping lists. The next step of my plan was to cook dishes that we were familiar with but fit within the new diet. The last steps will be trying new recipes and ingredients.

5.2 | Implement "**PROJECT**" Plan

Having a family plan is the same as having a project plan. I have developed an acronym to help you implement your plan and assist you in the process of reviewing and updating it as your family's needs and requirements change.

P   Plan

R   Requirements

O   Organize

J   January

E   Evaluate

C   Communicate

T   Time

P = Plan

Plan means that you have taken all of the things a family needs to plan for and divided them into different tasks, little buckets that you put together to create your plan. It is important to include all of the things you do in your family life—education, financial, medical, personal time, and weekly, yearly, and seasonal events, as well as the different ages of the kids in your family.

R = Requirements

Requirements include assessing your family's needs to make sure the tasks within the plan are supportive of those needs.

O = Organize

After you have your family requirements (needs), you have to organize those requirements into a plan, which means dividing them into buckets to utilize all the moments of time to get family tasks done.

J = January

Once a year, get together and update that plan with any family changes. For example, in January, start the year off with an updated plan.

E = Evaluate

The evaluation process doesn't only happen when you're putting together your parent plan the first time. It happens every year or season when you update your plan. If there are family emergencies or life changes, you'll need to update your plan, even if it's not time for your annual update in January. Another consideration is to evaluate priorities within each plan to label the high, medium, and low priorities. This will help with deciding which part of the plan to do first.

C = Communication

A plan is effective only when it is clearly communicated to all the family members and every family member has not only bought into it, but has a way to communicate their feedback and suggestions for changes, too.

T = Time

After you put together your project plan, you will be able to manage your time more efficiently by organizing the tasks you do in flexible timeframes (buckets). This will assist you as well in planning for what's ahead in order to reach your family goals and enjoy your family time.

CHAPTER SUMMARY

Creating plan documentation and how to implement the parent plan is key to its success. The acronym "PROJECT," P (Plan), R (Requirements), O (Organize), J (January/annual update), E (Evaluate), C (Communication) and—one of the most important thing that parents just can't get enough of—T (Time), is an easy way to remember how to implement your plan.

ABOUT THE AUTHOR

With three young boys (and a fabulous TechDad) in the home, Beth Blecherman transitioned from her position as Senior Manager at Deloitte to Family Manager for the Blecherman household. As the boys grew, Beth re-engaged her consulting career, using social media to discuss family technology. She is now applying her years of consulting, technology, and family management to help other families use project management and priority setting to create their own "Parent (PROJECT) Plan."

Beth Blecherman's personal blog, TechMamas.com, and her social media channels, including Twitter @TechMama, Google+, YouTube, and Facebook, offer tips, trends, and advice on all things concerning consumer electronics, apps, technology industry and social media. She also consults with companies on social media, product testing and analyzing trends for family technology. Beth has contributed family tech articles to multiple websites, including CoolMomTech.com, LaptopMag.com, and Mashable.com.

RESOURCES

Because technology is continually changing, it is difficult to include up-to-date technological websites, products, and resources in print. In order to provide my readers with the most current and up-to-date resources, I've included a list of these resources on my website, TechMamas.com. Please visit often to receive the latest technology-related information, products, and services for your family's evolving needs. Most important, we want to take the discussion online to build a Parent Plan community to discuss and share plans and strategies, so please stop by!

There are two ways to connect with TechMamas.com:

1. Connect with the TechMamas.com My Parent Plan resource page online using the following URL: http://techmamas.com/my-parent-plan-resources

2. Connect to the URL directly using the image on the next page from (currently) iOS (iTunes) and Android Devices (Google Play) using the Digimarc® Discover app http://www.digimarc.com/discover/the-digimarc-discover-app

Check the Digimarc website for full device compatibility details and instructions.

CPSIA information can be obtained at www.ICGtesting.com
Printed in the USA
BVOW09s1656101114

374459BV00022B/455/P

9 781492 147091